The Little Boat

by

Rachael Bae

This book is dedicated to:

GOD, who saw fit to give me the idea to write this story.

Mom, for nurturing my love of books from an early age by reading to me until her voice went hoarse.

And **Dad**, for all his support and encouragement. Thanks for the "recharge", Daddykins!

THE LITTLE BOAT
Copyright © Rachael Bae, 2021
Printed in the USA. All Rights Reserved.
ISBN: 978-1-7376412-0-9

SPECIAL EDITION FOR PLAZA VISTA SCHOOL

"A new commandment I give to you, that you love one another: just as I have loved you, you also are to love one another."
(John 13:34 ESV)

In a town not far from here, where the seagulls swoop across the glittering bay, and the dock smells of salt with moldy fish...

There was a little boat.

The *Little Boat* was smaller than many of the other boats in the dock, insignificant next to the usefulness of a fishing boat or the luxury of a fancy yacht.

Every day, he would watch the other boats leave the dock and return with exciting tales of the world beyond the bay. He was in awe of them, and admired their bravery very much.

Some shared stories of giant fish
caught on flying lines,
and the dangers of going out
to the rougher waters.

Others gushed about the beautiful sunsets
that could only be seen clearly on the other side of town.
They told of all the parties and celebrations
that had been held on their decks.

There were even boats that were taken out amongst sharks with razor sharp teeth,

whales that sprayed them with showers of salty water,

and pods of friendly dolphins.

The other boats were kind and caring. They knew the *Little Boat* would be too small and weak in the face of the currents that chopped against their sides outside of the bay.

To lessen his want for adventure,
the other boats tried to make
their stories seem more boring,
and often refused to tell him stories at all.

please, please, PLEASE?

Still, the *Little Boat* hungered to see the world.
A long time passed, but he had not been taken out of the dock even once.
It was just when he had almost lost all hope that everything changed.

One bright and early morning,
a family approached the dock.
The mother and father chatted happily,
watching their children enjoy
the fresh ocean breeze.

The *Little Boat* bobbed hopefully in the water as they came closer and closer to him. Would this be his chance?

To the surprise of all the boats, the family climbed aboard his deck and untied him from the dock.

Despite their worries, the other boats rocked side to side encouragingly.

As they cast off, the *Little Boat* began to imagine
what kind of adventure he would be going on.

Would he brave tall, crashing waves,
painted blue and green and gold under the sun?

Would the shimmering fish greet him
on his first trip past the bay?

Would he weather
sudden, terrible
storms and heroically
bring his passengers back
to the safety of calm waters?

He imagined how it would feel
to finally see a sunset, with red, orange,
and pink splashes painting the sky...

None of that happened.
The family sailed him inside the bay,
drifting along with the breeze.
Seagulls flew above him,
squawking and making loopty-loops,
as if they were mocking him
with their freedom.

The *Little Boat* was flooded with disappointment.
He had dreamed of having a grand adventure for so long,
but they were just taking him out for a boring sail.

But right when he began to sulk over his misfortune,
he noticed the family's faces.
Pure love brightened each and every one of them
as they enjoyed the happiness of simply
being together under the gentle sunlight,
lulled by the soft swell of the ocean.

The *Little Boat* saw how the mother
pressed a kiss to her son's forehead.
He saw the father ruffle his daughter's windswept hair.
He saw the siblings bump shoulders and laugh together.
He saw the father drape a coat over his wife's back,
and saw the mother press her hand against her husband's.

The *Little Boat* felt a warm glow spread within him.
Suddenly, the need for adventure didn't seem
so important anymore.
Nothing in the other boats' stories could ever compare
to the sight of this family just loving each other.

SQUAK!
SQUAK!

The day ended all too quickly,
but the *Little Boat* gladly went back
to the dock.
He had seen the most beautiful sight of all,
and he couldn't wait to tell the others.

So in that town not too far from here,
where the seagulls swoop across the bay,
and the dock smells of salt with moldy fish...

Even now,
the *Little Boat* waits
with an eager heart
for the next family
to come his way.

Author's Note

I wrote this book for several reasons. This may be a children's book, but the lessons are those that all of us should take to heart.

All throughout their lives, people search for meaning and purpose. We fear that we are too insignificant, too small in this world to ever do anything that means something.

This first lesson is one that I've struggled with for a long time, and still do. As a disabled individual, I've often wondered if I'll ever be able to make a difference in the world. The *Little Boat* is the smallest boat in the dock, weak and plain, but he proves that we all have a purpose, no matter what size or shape. It may not be some grand plan where you improve the lives of millions—or maybe it is, who knows!—but it doesn't have to be. Sometimes, the simplest things are what we treasure the most.

It can be hard to remember what's important in this life, with all the distractions we have vying for our attention on a day to day basis, especially in the midst of this pandemic. I'm no exception; like many others, I prioritize things that I perhaps ought not to, whether it's money and recognition, or something simple as video games. On their own, none of those things are exactly bad, just like how the *Little Boat*'s longing for adventure isn't bad at all. It is only detrimental if they become our idols.

The lesson that the *Little Boat* learns is one I have learned and relearned every day of my life—it's the importance of family. Of all the amazing parts of this world, family is the most essential. There are always exceptions, but most families love, nurture, and teach each other. This is what's so beautiful: the human connection, or more specifically, familial connection.

The world has become increasingly more selfish as the years go by. It's all *me, me, me, what can I do for me and only me*, and sometimes it's even glorified. Whether it's taking that last ice cream when you know your dad likes it too and would probably like to have it after a stressful day at work (I *know* I've done that at some point), or tucking your wallet away in your pocket when you pass by a homeless person on the sidewalk. It's not wrong to want nice things, or to go after what you want, but we should also take the time to direct our attention to people around us.

The final lesson that the *Little Boat* learns is the joy of kindness, without any expectations for what you can gain. When the family first takes him for a sail, he's disappointed. His focus was solely on what he could experience for himself, the things he thought would satisfy him, but soon realized that doing something to bring happiness to others is the true gift. We should also recognize that in a society that has become so divided, you and I must be the first to take a step forward and put out a helping hand.

The author and the illustrator, Rachael and Ananya, are longtime friends who attend the same high school in Southern California.
Rachael loves writing stories, and Ananya is a great artist, so they did their best to put their two talents together to create this picture book!